HOW TO DRAW FIGURES IN ACTION

THE HOW TO DRAW *SERIES*

- D. C. SHARP.

JUNE 1953 -

HOW TO DRAW
FIGURES IN ACTION
by
CHARLES WOOD

THE STUDIO: LONDON & NEW YORK

First printed   1948
Reprinted   1953

*Printed in England by Bradford & Dickens,
Drayton House, W.C.1, and published in London
by The Studio Limited, 66 Chandos Place, W.C.2.
and in New York by The Studio Publications Inc.,
432 Fourth Avenue.*

CONTENTS

INTRODUCTION

This book, my second in the ' How to Draw ' series, is intended to help and encourage the student into the more adventurous field of illustrative art.

I am assuming from the start that the reader has some knowledge of drawing. In a book of this size it is, of course, impossible to deal with all the aspects of training in the drawing of the human figure, such as anatomy. There are many excellent books on this subject obtainable from your local public library should you wish to study it. Some people maintain that a knowledge of anatomy is not essential, but personally, I believe that the more one knows of a subject the better ; after all it is part of one's equipment.

To put movement into a figure one must draw from memory, I say memory, rather than imagination, because one draws upon one's experience when conjuring up a pose in the mind's eye. This being the case, let us then resolve to observe people more closely and carry a sketch book in which to draw rough notes of poses which interest us.

When I first draw a figure in a required pose, I usually like to refer to a model. First I decide on the sort of action I want, by means of a few quick sketches and then, while drawing it in, I check up, as it were, by getting one of my family or friends to take up the position, or parts of it—perhaps a foreshortened arm or unusual angle of the head.

Get yourself a drawing pad or book of thinnish paper and draw as often as you can. I would suggest a fairly soft pencil and plastic rubber, if you can get it. Don't be ashamed to rub out and start again—it helps you to get your hand and brain working together.

Some people have a natural gift for putting things down as they see them, but this does not mean that they are drawing expressively or even well. A camera can record what it sees, but what the camera sees is merely superficial, whereas the artist can, if he knows what to go for, produce something that lives.

In my book 'How to Draw Portraits' I have endeavoured to show the reader how to construct. In this one I have tried to show how the lines of construction and those of rhythmic action can be used to the same purpose, enabling the student to state the active pose from the first stages of the drawing, maintaining it to the finish. In the next chapter I am dealing with a problem which, to my mind, has had far too little attention.

Let us start with transitory movement. By that, I mean the incidental things people do at a time when no positive action is taking place. Two people talking perhaps. The first thing one imagines is a couple of figures standing, looking at each other. Certainly not a subject for movement; too static, we say. Let us watch two people talking. A man and a woman. The woman adjusts the position of the handbag under her arm, changes her weight on to the other foot and places one hand on her hip. The man tilts his head sideways a little, taps his pipe bowl downwards on the palm of his hand, moving his arms to the side as he does so. All this takes only a minute or two and each of these movements alters the attitudes so that they are never at any time standing stiffly facing each other.

If we consider these things before actually committing ourselves to pencil and paper we can choose the most interesting aspect of a given situation.

The more definite actions, such as pouring out the coffee or drawing the curtains can always be illustrated much more effectively if the artist either goes through the movements himself, in front of a mirror, or asks someone else to perform them.

Regarding the more vigorous forms of movement : I have dealt with these at length, endeavouring at the same time to guide the student in such matters as choosing the best viewpoint and the making of a picture.

I would just like to stress one point, *i.e.* that vigorous action is not the only kind of movement that is interesting to draw.

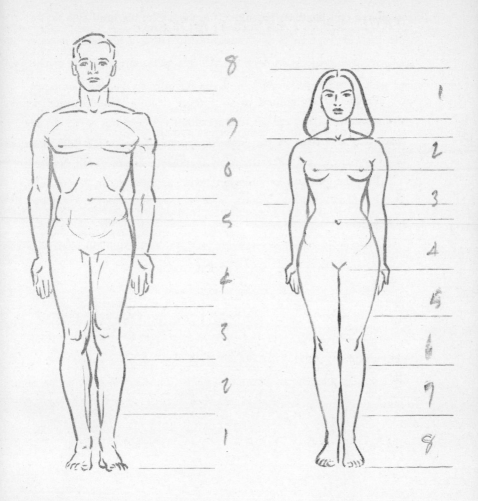

8

7

6

5

4

3

2

1

1

2

3

4

5

6

7

8

9

TRUE SPONTANEOUS MOVEMENT

People we see around us are forever striking attitudes, even the sitting ones. If they are not they are either selfconscious or ill. In any case, we, as artists, at the moment pursuing the delightful subject of ' movement,' are interested only in poses that are worth drawing.

For the purpose of ' blocking out,' scribbling, or, if you like,

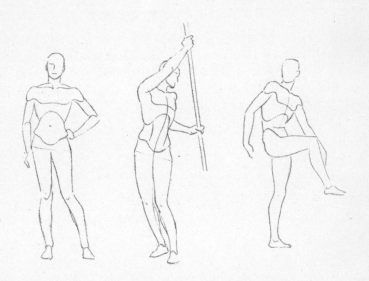

'thinking on paper,' I have suggested a few symbols, a sort of short-hand, so that we can put in a rough figure without having to bother prematurely with details.

I have also suggested two fairly average figures, one male and the other female, and divided them up into various proportions. These symbolic figure shapes, together with the proportions, can help you to work out your poses more freely than if you were to start drawing from the head downwards. If you did this you would not only get your sketch out of proportion but you would lose the spirit of the pose.

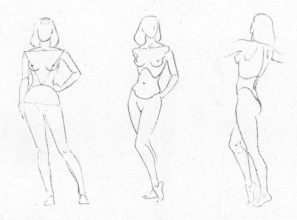

A child does not sit like this when reading a book. The figures below were sketched from life. The little girl was given a book to look at and she wriggled into at least half a dozen different positions (each successive one more comfortable no doubt) within five minutes. The more comfortable poses are the nicest to draw.

The little girl, having shifted into this final position, has automatically adjusted her weight so that it is evenly " balanced." See how the foot is placed forward to take some of the weight off the elbows. This is how I usually start.

TENDENCY TO UNDERSTATE

Even when we like a pose and decide to draw it we are sometimes inclined to straighten up the angles and curves, usually due to a kind of nervousness. This failing occurs especially where the figure is bending down.

The best way to combat this is to first put in the main lines of the action as I have suggested a little further on in this book.

A caricaturist is very bold—he even overstates the truth. I have found, however, that often when I think I have overstated I have not done so at all, but merely looked more deeply. Try this and I think you too will find it so.

When a pose is correctly drawn and the angles and rhythm are correctly observed it looks easy and convincing. If this were not so it would not be a pleasing drawing.

Carry a sketch book with you.

15

Rhythm and balance are very closely allied. When I draw an upright figure I put a vertical line through it from head to foot. When I draw from a model I hold my pencil vertically between my eye and the model. By this process I am able to judge more accurately the angle of the head, body and limbs.

RHYTHM

AND BALANCE

These are rough charcoal sketches. They are not drawn from models but worked out on the following principle.

First I try to imagine how the action I want could be represented in lines rather like bent wire. These lines we will call the ' basic lines,' those on which the pose is built. This is not a trick or easy way of drawing but a means of arriving at the very essence of the action of the action which is taking place.

These lines are far more important than the expression on the child's face.

If we were to start at the top of the head and work down we might find ourselves absorbed in such details as facial expression, losing sight of the rhythm and grace of the movement.

Now see if you can find the basic lines as shown here. Just
place a piece of paper at the bottom of pages 18, 19 and 20.

Then try some poses of your own. I'm sure you will not find it difficult.

If you work out your sketches in this manner you will find you can, after a while, visualise any pose you want, and, if you are not sure of the way a hand or leg goes you can check up by getting a friend to pose for you.

I mentioned in my introduction one or two things about people talking and the movements they make. If you were an illustrator you would find that most of the situations you were asked to illustrate would be, not exciting, but more or less tame ones, such as " ' Let me lend you the money ' said Janet." In this case I would draw Janet, one hand on a convenient chair-back or table, leaning forward impulsively. This movement, besides expressing the spirit of the text, at once makes Janet the centre of interest. One must get as much out of the situation as possible to make the illustration interesting.

On the opposite page I have shown some men in conversational attitudes. Make a point of observing people as they really are ; the gestures they make and the attitudes they strike will register themselves on your memory, to be conjured up at will.

Twists and turns of the head and body play an integral part in natural rhythmic movement. These men are just doubting, acquiescing, emphasising, etc., but there is movement in their attitudes.

24

VIGOROUS ACTION

I would like to emphasise the need for what is sometimes called artist's licence. To demonstrate, I have used on the following page a more or less accurate copy of a photograph of a man kicking a football. In this sketch I have merely copied—a shameful thing for an artist to do, isn't it ?

There is no harm in using photographic reference so long as you do ' use ' it. A camera cannot possibly be expected to do anything more than catch a glimpse of the whole movement.   When we draw the footballer however, we are helped by looking at the photographic reference (not forgetting to go through the motion to get the feeling of the thing) to visualise the action at its best. So, by accentuating, rather than exaggerating, we can produce a much livelier picture,

In the sketch opposite I have stressed those lines which travel in an upward curve, giving the figure as much swing as possible.

'COPIED' FROM A PHOTOGRAPH

A photograph, though sometimes very useful, always gives me the impression of "arrested" action, whereas, with a drawing, the artist,

'DRAWN' FROM THE SAME PHOTOGRAPH

having chosen the most expressive stage of the whole movement, can convey a feeling of actual energetic effort.

VITAL SIMPLICITY

This is very important. Any little detail that happens to interrupt a line or curve, I would leave out, or at least make as little of it as possible. There are, of course, occasions when leaving out is impossible —the contour of the arm, for instance, must be anatomically correct. But even so, it may still be arranged to conform to the desired curve. If you have looked at Botticelli's paintings, you will have noticed a

First scribble, feeling our way.

Drawing the stretched folds helps to give the movement.

See how the tennis player flings out his left arm to help maintain his balance. He is leaping sideways. A fast thinking movement. All the time he is on the alert, having to spring in any direction at a second's notice.

beautiful rippling movement in the drapery which suggests an ethereal lightness, as though a gentle wind were rustling through the flimsy material. These figures are moving gracefully, gently, almost gliding. Drapery has a wonderful capacity for showing both form and movement, and Botticelli's paintings have derived much of their beauty from. its use. Michelangelo and Rubens, among others, clothed moving figures in flowing draperies, although they conveyed a more robust and lively movement. By the use of these draperies the old masters linked up the figures in their compositions making beautiful and colourful patterns. The clothes men wear nowadays are prosaic by comparison, and even the women's fashions are not always inspiring to those who would express modern figures in motion ; but there is beauty in almost any graceful moving form however it is covered.

Earlier in the book, I asked you to search for basic lines ; these are very evident in the movements of dancing figures. Dancers study the science of rhythmical movement. They learn to leap, twist and turn so that their bodies conform to delightful rhythmic shapes. It is possible to trace the curves and angles suggested ; to analyse and draw them as lines upon which the whole figure may be built.

The more we simplify these lines the nearer we get to the truth of the movement. We can also be more direct in our rendering and more certain of what we are attempting to convey. Thus, by getting to the root, as it were, of the subject, we are able to work with assurance, producing a direct interpretation.

This is a flying, leaping motion in which the drapery swirls in lovely shapes. Notice how the head goes back, carrying on the curve of the body and right leg. The arms and left leg seem to support rather than detract from the main rhythm.

Notice here, how the curve of the arms balances the curve of the body and legs.

The dancer here has
sprung upward onto her
toes. The whole move-
ment is that of an
upward sweep.

33

c

SYSTEM OF FOLDS

In the preceding chapters, I have spoken of the value of drapery as an aid to the artistic expression of the movements of the form it covers.

After drawing figures from life, in various types of costume, it becomes apparent to the student that folds in all kinds of material have a systematic action, which is the result of several forces of influence.

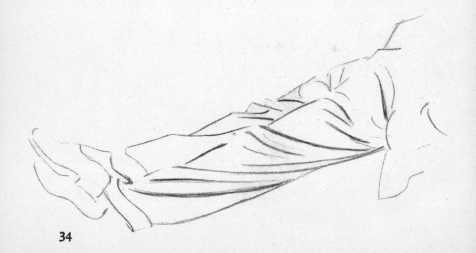

One, the material draped loosely, tends to fall in gentle curves ; two, when stretched as when the form underneath is suddenly moved forward or upright, the curves straighten out and the tighter the pull the straighter the fold ; three, the tendency to radiate from the source of the pull, as do the folds in a sleeve when the arm is lifted. Then there is the falling of drapery, a sort of collapsing, floating movement, and the quality it has of suggesting the form it covers. Examples are shown on the following pages.

By studying these influences then, we can eventually apply to the purpose of drawing from memory the knowledge of the principles.

This leg indicates repose. The folds are gentler, not stretched vigorously as in the case of the arm shown overloaf.

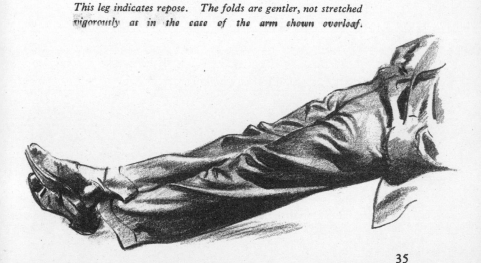

Here is an arm upraised. Here the contours and solid forms are indicated by shading.

Notice how the folds radiate from the armpit, and help to convey the solid arm and its outer shape.

36

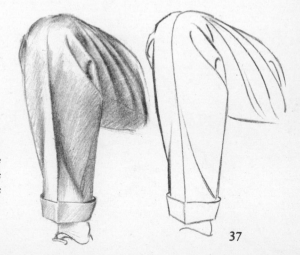

Folds express form as movement. Where the material is stretched, the folds are firmer than those formed by the material hanging suspended.

The lines and folds still radiate from the tightest part and it is easy to see where the cloth is actually touching the leg.

37

Brush & ink

These are just a few simple diagrams to show the type of movements to draw for exercises. The best way to learn about drapery is to draw it constantly.

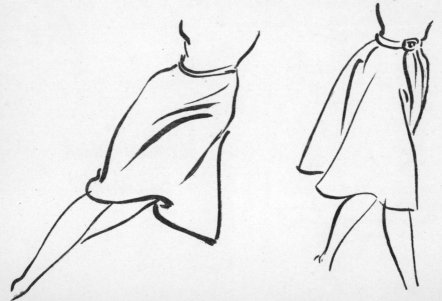

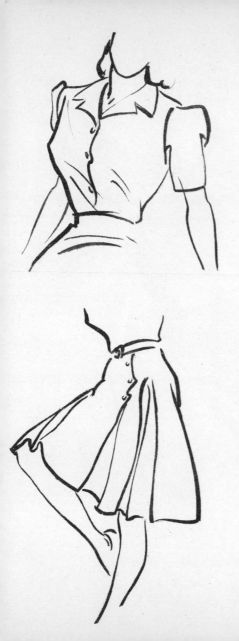

A few quick
Studies

39

THE GOALKEEPER "FLINGS HIMSELF INTO SPACE"

FIGURES THAT MIGHT TUMBLE

It is just as well to dwell, for a moment, on the subject of figures that are obviously flinging themselves into space, without the calculated forethought which is necessary to land them on their feet.

When jumping an obstacle, we instinctively adjust ourselves so that our weight is properly distributed to maintain our balance. Whichever way we jump, sometimes with arms and feet thrust forward or with the upward sweep of the legs and roll of the body over the stick in the high jump, we take into account the eventual landing.

That is when we jump *over* something. There are times, however, when this question of landing safely is overshadowed by a more urgent purpose. When we leap to catch a ball or to clutch a branch we keep our mind on our hands instead of our feet, so that, should we miscalculate, we land more often than not in a sprawling attitude.

All the the effort displayed here is in the upper
part of the figure, the legs have been used to
give the upward spring and are now relaxed.

Goalkeeper leaps and twists. He sees the ball coming for the corner of the goal; he has to leap sideways to catch it but cannot take his eyes off it.

WALL

PROP

PROP

USING A MODEL

For this chapter I have chosen a rather difficult subject—a man falling off a roof—to demonstrate how problems of this sort can be overcome.

This incident was chosen at random. I tried to think of something thrilling and dramatic and this was the result. I scribbled about, trying this angle and that, until I decided upon a slightly overhead view, so that I could get the atmosphere of falling and height ; looking down a huge well between tall buildings into a street dotted with small figures and cars. Atmospheric possibilities are numerous and varied, and can be of intrinsic value when properly considered.

Having followed my process of thought the reader will see that I have not only decided on the position of the figure, but also on the best way to present it.

This matter is dealt with on earlier pages. Having made up my mind as to the attitude of the falling man (after shutting my eyes and trying to imagine myself in the position of the falling person), I tried actually falling backwards, and found that I instinctively flung out one hand behind me while I clutched at the air with the other.

As this is to be an illustration of the ' close up ' variety I must, of course, put in a good deal of detail, still treating the sketch as broadly and simply as possible. This meant that I must either rely on my memory and work out the incidental details such as the folds in the clothes by a kind of trial and error process, or use a model. I decided on the latter course.

As it is not possible to suspend a person in mid-air, I had to arrange my model and my point of view to suit the case.

Most of my friends are good friends. I am sure of this because most of them have, at some time or other, undergone the most severe tests at my bidding. They have all posed for me from time to time and as they still venture into my studio I must assume that their friendship

FALLING FIGURES

ROUGH SKETCHES

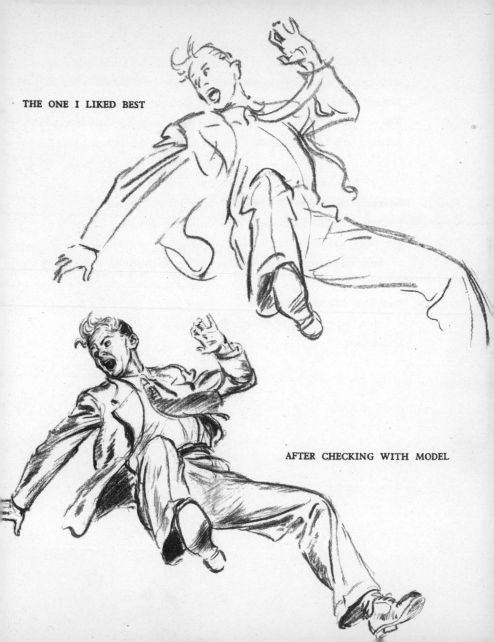

THE ONE I LIKED BEST

AFTER CHECKING WITH MODEL

still prevails. I'm sure we all have friends like these who are only waiting to be asked. It was one of these kind people who allowed himself to be placed on the floor, one arm propped on a chair and one · foot supported by some books. The flying coat tails, however, had to be imagined and the trouser legs needed some attention to make them ' move.'

I then did a rough charcoal sketch, shown on page 44. Several sketches, two of which are reproduced on page 46, were scrapped because I felt that this was one of those instances where the reader of the story was to be made to share as much as possible the feelings of the falling man. The reader is looking from above, and I felt that if I failed to show the man's face with his expression of terror I should lessen the dramatic effect.

On page 57 I have shown the rough composition for the complete illustration.

DECORATIVE GROUP FOR A POSTER

Among my readers there are, no doubt, many potential poster-artists—most artists, whether or not they are commercial, are interested in good posters—hence the inclusion of this chapter.

In twenty years poster design has made tremendous progress, and at its best it now ranks as a high form of art. The poster still ' tells a story ' but to-day design demands that its lines shall convey its message in simple, direct and forceful fashion. Seen from the opposite side of the street, its very pattern should attract and hold the attention, even at that distance making its message clear.

To-day, also, the industrial artist has much control in production and reproduction and plans his designs so that they benefit fully from the various techniques employed. The idea for a poster is usually conceived by a ' visualiser ' in an advertising agency. He specialises in ideas and design. He executes a ' rough ' which is usually just scribble showing the space occupied by the lettering and text matter and the general shape of the illustration.

Sometimes a more finished rough is made as a guide to general effect including, perhaps, the colour scheme. I have used for this example the working drawings that were executed by me for an actual poster.

Yellow
buff

Red

Dark
Green

RCA
Tacket

Lighter
Purkies

Grey
Skirt

50

The scribble that was sent to me was just an indication of the shape to which the figures were to conform. My job then was to fit three figures of young housewives in brightly coloured clothes. Notice how the very shape suggests an intimate whispering group. To make the figures as attractive as possible I had to imagine the most interesting attitudes possible within the bounds of the design.

Just a few " thumbnails." We seldom decide at once what we want to portray.

We might prefer an overhead view indicating height by the very small figures below, or the lower view conveying the impression of oncoming speed.

In all cases the other shapes in the picture must help, by their weight and direction, to give speed to the figure.

ROUGH COMPOSITIONS

As you are no doubt aware, composition is the most important consideration in a picture. No matter how excellent the draughtsmanship or how delightful the colour, if the composition is bad, the picture is bad.

I have already mentioned in this book that a design, for that is what a composition is, should be pleasing to the eye for its own sake. In other words, one should not have to peer closely at a picture in order to become interested. The very shapes of tones and their values in relation to each other should please and interest. How often have we done a rough tone sketch only to spoil it later by adding too much fussy detail. It is easy to see why this happens. A sketch broadly conceived and freely rendered, has genuine feeling. The right amounts of light tone, dark tone, middle tone, and black and white are instinctively balanced.

While it is necessary, in most cases, to put some detail into a picture we must be careful not to destroy the effect we have achieved in the rough by cutting up those broad tone patterns with little bits of light and dark.

Supposing we have two squares, one is light grey in tone, and the other dark grey. Each square is in contrast to the other. Now let us stipple dark dots on the light square, and light dots on the dark one. This done, the contrast is no longer evident ; the tone effect becomes similar. This is what happens when we add finishing touches without the right amount of thought and consideration ; the picture becomes drab and insipid.

There are other qualities necessary to constitute a good composition, such as movement and rhythm. Rhythm suggests movement.

Rhythm in composition is no new idea, it is as old as painting itself. The great painters used it in the murals and in cathedral domes ; angels with streaming draperies ; groups of figures designed to lead the eye to the main interest in the picture ; clouds sweeping across the skies. Their pictures were abundant with rhythm. No doubt the student is already aware of the amount of knowledge to be gained from the great masters, but just in case there should be some readers who have hitherto had little opportunity for study, let me urge them to borrow books and go to art galleries.

DRAMATIC SENSE

There are many ways of describing an incident, and some are better than others. The artist has an advantage over the storyteller, inasmuch as he is able to take you to the scene and let you see it for yourself. Earlier on, I decided to use the subject of the falling man as a demonstration. There is rather more in this question than choosing the viewpoint, if we are to convey the feeling of dangerous height.

On the next page I have worked out two charcoal roughs using the same figure, but with two very different viewpoints. The first one, to me, is quite dramatic, but rather reminiscent of a comedy film—after all there may be another roof a few feet below for him to fall on to!

Then there is another point about composition No. 1; it doesn't awaken any familiar feeling of fear does it? We have, most of us, looked up at the high diving board at a swimming pool and fancied ourselves joyously executing graceful swallow dives, but when we have mounted the steps and stood looking down, we have undergone a change of view in more senses than one. So to get the true feeling of height we must 'get up there.'

In composition No. 2 I have done this by showing the street far below, which, I think does arouse those familiar feelings. Even the strongest people experience a thrill of some sort or another when they look down from a height. The figure is now in its right atmosphere.

This sketch shows only the beginning of a nasty fall. He might, however, be lucky enough to fall onto another roof a few feet below.

This situation is much more dramatic. The reader can
see for himself, so to speak, because he's on the spot.

Here are two different presentations of the same illustration: the pirate is stealing furtively away with the treasure tightly clutched under one arm. He has a pistol too. He is not a prepossessing character. He strikes an ominous note. The whole figure must be stealthy and portentous. Even the shadows on the landscape and the way the moon is suggested in the sky must be in key with the figure which lurks there in semi-silhouette.

The incident has dramatic possibilities. In the first picture I have not stressed these things. I have purposely avoided the possibilities and tried to produce just the effect one would get through timidity of approach.

As it is a moonlight scene the tones must be on the dark side. It would not be practicable to do the sketch and just put a dark wash of grey over the whole area. That would simply result in the picture becoming a drab and uninteresting one. After drawing out the figure one might be reluctant to sacrifice the nice effect achieved in the drawing itself, but this quality is purely incidental and not nearly so important as the main effect of the whole design. The same applies to the cliffs, the sea and the ship. These details however interesting individually must not be allowed to obtrude.

If you compare the two you will, I think, agree that the second is the more effective. The movement of the figure, which is of the utmost importance has to be decided on from the start ; another fact that had to be considered was that it was an illustration to appeal to boys and therefore had to possess a certain romantic quality, almost a theatrical atmosphere. Notice the slinking furtiveness of the pose.

Never be afraid of getting the most out of a situation and remember that a figure always has *some* movement.

CHOOSING THE ANGLE OR VIEWPOINT

If you were an illustrator your main job would be to present pictorially an incident in a story. Quite often, the editor will stipulate the situation he wants illustrated. This can be very disappointing to an artist who, having read the typescript, really feels he could get more enthusiastic over another incident, perhaps one with more action or more drama in it.

Now if you found yourself in a similar position and approached the editor, stating your feelings in the matter, that gentleman would quite likely tell you to go ahead and make a nice job of it.

However, sometimes the editor has a definite reason for selecting a particular scene to be illustrated, and in such case the artist must endeavour to create his own drama and action.

It is possible to make a dramatic composition out of practically any incident, by arranging your figures and your masses of tone so that they make exciting shapes in themselves. You would, most probably, be given the required size and shape, and, as the layout of the book would probably have been planned beforehand, you would be expected to adhere to it.

Let us suppose you were given a Western story to illustrate, the incident being one in which the hero is seated at a table on which is a drink and some playing cards. The door of the shack is suddenly kicked open and the outlaw appears, menacing, holding a gun.

There are several ways of picturing such a scene. Firstly, as the situation is tense, you must be as dramatic as possible. Secondly, you must choose your viewpoint. The hero might be viewed close up, with the outlaw framed in the doorway, or better, the menacing figure of the villain could dominate the picture. He could be semi-silhouetted, which would strengthen the overpowering shape. The hero, on the other hand, is taken by surprise, he is at a disadvantage, he is being menaced, so by making the outlaw the larger of the two, by placing him in the foreground, the right atmosphere is created.

These problems should be worked out on paper, by means of
several pencil or charcoal scribbles, or, to use a more professional
term 'roughs.' This practice enlarges your imaginative scope, and
helps you to visualise the movement.